SUPER
FACTS
FOR SUPER KIDS

FIVE
SUPER
FACT-FILLED
BOOKS!

Ready-to-Re

T0014893

Simon Spotlight
New York   London   Toronto   Sydney   New Delhi

INCLUDES:

TIGERS CAN'T PURR!
AND OTHER AMAZING FACTS

SHARKS CAN'T SMILE!
AND OTHER AMAZING FACTS

POLAR BEAR FUR ISN'T WHITE!
AND OTHER AMAZING FACTS

SNAKES SMELL WITH THEIR TONGUES!
AND OTHER AMAZING FACTS

ALLIGATORS AND CROCODILES CAN'T CHEW!
AND OTHER AMAZING FACTS

SIMON SPOTLIGHT
An imprint of Simon & Schuster Children's Publishing Division
1230 Avenue of the Americas, New York, New York 10020
This Simon Spotlight paperback edition May 2024
Tigers Can't Purr! © 2020 by Simon & Schuster, LLC; by Thea Feldman;
illustrated by Lee Cosgrove; stock photos by iStock.
Sharks Can't Smile! © 2020 by Simon & Schuster, LLC; by Elizabeth Dennis;
illustrated by Lee Cosgrove; stock photos by iStock and Shutterstock.
Polar Bear Fur Isn't White! © 2020 by Simon & Schuster, LLC; by Thea Feldman;
illustrated by Lee Cosgrove; stock photos by iStock.
Snakes Smell With Their Tongues! © 2021 by Simon & Schuster, LLC; by Thea Feldman;
illustrated by Lee Cosgrove; stock photos by iStock.
Alligators and Crocodiles Can't Chew! © 2021 by Simon & Schuster, LLC; by Thea Feldman;
illustrated by Lee Cosgrove; stock photos by iStock.
Simon & Schuster: Celebrating 100 Years of Publishing in 2024
For information about special discounts for bulk purchases, please contact
Simon & Schuster Special Sales at 1-866-506-1949
or business@simonandschuster.com.
Manufactured in Malaysia 0124 SCP
2 4 6 8 10 9 7 5 3 1
ISBN 978-1-6659-5943-8 (pbk)
ISBN 978-1-5344-6776-7 (*Tigers Can't Purr!* ebook)
ISBN 978-1-5344-6773-6 (*Sharks Can't Smile!* ebook)
ISBN 978-1-5344-7665-3 (*Polar Bear Fur Isn't White!* ebook)
ISBN 978-1-5344-8523-5 (*Snakes Smell with Their Tongues!* ebook)
ISBN 978-1-5344-7981-4 (*Alligators and Crocodiles Can't Chew!* ebook)
These titles were previously published individually by Simon Spotlight with slightly different text and art.

TIGERS CAN'T PURR!
AND OTHER AMAZING FACTS

GLOSSARY

apex predator: an animal who is not eaten or hunted by other animals in the wild

camouflage: when an animal uses its natural colors or traits to hide in its surroundings

chuff: to push air out through the nostrils to show excitement and greet other tigers

endangered: at risk of disappearing forever

extinct: no longer existing on Earth

grasslands: large open areas covered in grass

habitat: the natural environment where an animal lives

predator: an animal who hunts, kills, and eats other animals

prey: an animal hunted by a predator

recycled: made from materials that have been used before

retractable: able to be pulled back in

territory: an area of land that animals claim for themselves

Note to readers: Some of these words may have more than one definition. The definitions above match how these words are used in this book.

Tigers are super.

They can climb tall trees

and roar as loud as jet planes.

There's one thing that tigers

cannot do, though . . . purr!

By the time you get to the tail end of this book, you'll know all about what makes tigers amazing!

CHAPTER 1

TOP HUNTERS

There are six types of tigers in the world.

 **Siberian**
(say: Sai-BEER-ee-uhn)

 **Bengal**
(say: BEN-gull)

 **Indochinese**
(say: IN-doe-chai-NEEZ)

 **Sumatran**
(say: soo-MAH-truhn)

 **Malayan**
(say: muh-LAY-uhn)

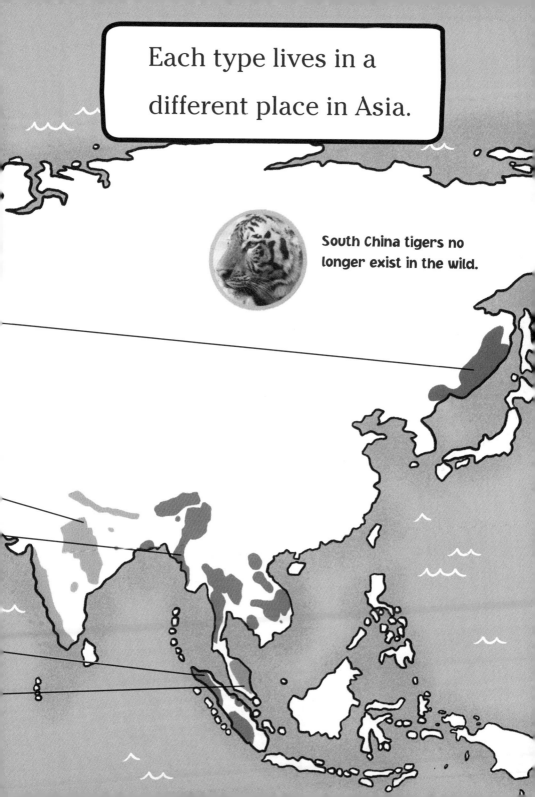

Each type lives in a different place in Asia.

South China tigers no longer exist in the wild.

Siberian tigers mostly live in cold and snowy forests.
Other tigers live in hot and swampy habitats (say: HA-bih-tats), or homes.
Some live in dry grasslands and rain forests, too.

DEER

WATER BUFFALO

CROCODILE

All tigers are predators
(say: PRED-uh-turz),
which means they hunt and eat
other animals called prey
(say: PRAY).
Their prey includes deer,
water buffalo, and even
other predators like crocodiles!

Tigers hunt about once a week
and can eat up to 88 pounds
of food when they are hungry.
That is heavier than 350 bananas!
They sometimes bury the leftovers
and dig them up to eat later.

Tigers are called apex (say: AY-pecks) or top predators because they aren't hunted or eaten by any other animals in the wild. For example, insects are eaten by wild pigs, who in turn are eaten by Bengal tigers. Since no one eats tigers, they are apex predators . . . one of the top hunters in the world!

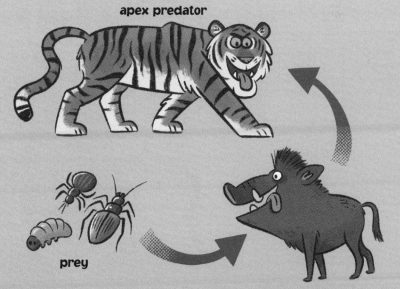

apex predator

prey

insect predator and tiger prey

CHAPTER 2

TERRIFIC FROM HEAD TO TAIL

When you imagine tigers, you probably first think of their bold stripes. Each tiger has its own pattern of stripes.

If you ever shaved a tiger's fur, you'd discover that it even has stripes on its skin!

The thin stripes help tigers blend in to the thin shadows of tall grass, making it hard to spot them.

Now you see me, now you don't...

This ability to blend in and hide is called camouflage (say: KAM-uh-flahj).

Siberian tigers are bigger than any other cat in the world. They can grow up to about 10 feet long and weigh as much as 660 pounds.

That means a Siberian tiger is longer than two and a half male Great Danes . . . and heavier than five of them!

660 pounds

600 pounds

POLAR BEARS: UP TO 1,600 POUNDS

BROWN BEARS: UP TO 1,500 POUNDS

TIGERS: UP TO 660 POUNDS

LIONS: UP TO 500 POUNDS

CHEETAHS: UP TO 145 POUNDS

HOUSE CATS: UP TO 20 POUNDS

In fact, polar bears and brown bears are the only predators on land larger than Siberian tigers.

Human: up to 27.8 miles per hour

20 30 35 40

Tiger: up to 40 miles per hour

Don't let a tiger's large size fool you into thinking it moves slowly, though. They can run up to 40 miles per hour, which is faster than the fastest human ever!

Tigers have long hind legs, which help them push hard off the ground and leap up to 30 feet.

That's half the length of a bowling lane!

Here's something else that's terrific about tigers.

They can move very quietly, thanks to retractable claws that they can pull back into their toes. This way, the claws don't hit against the ground and make noise when they walk.

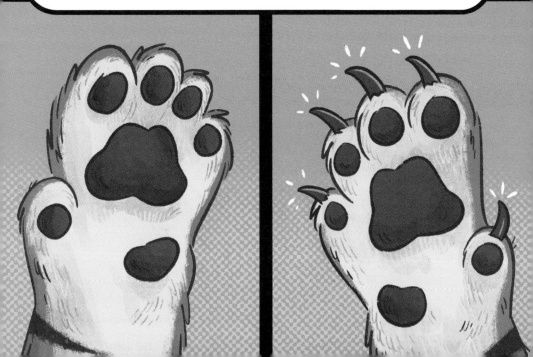

Tigers also have padding

on their paws that muffle sounds.

Tigers don't see clearly for the first few weeks of their lives. But adult tigers can see about 6 times better in the dark than most humans.

Tigers also hear better than humans, and can turn their ears in different directions to focus on specific sounds. All these skills are helpful for tigers to catch prey!

NOT A HOUSE CAT!

Tigers might look like giant house cats, but they differ in many ways. For example, tigers can't purr! Scientists believe tigers can't purr because of extra tissue in their throats.

Tigers may not be able to purr . . . but they can ROAR!

Tigers also hiss, growl, groan, and grunt.

Mothers moan to their cubs to get their attention.

Tigers chuff to greet one another, and when they are excited.

Chuffing is when tigers close their mouths and push air out through their nostrils.

Tigers don't just "talk" to other tigers with their voices. Male tigers declare their territory, an area they want to claim as their own, by scratching their claws on trees and the ground.

They also rub their faces or spray their urine against rocks and trees in the territory.

All these marks and scents tell other tigers to "Stay away!"

EWW!

Tigers and house cats are also different when it comes to water. Most house cats hate getting wet, but tigers like it! They go into rivers and lakes to cool off.

Tigers are also great swimmers and can swim up to 5 miles.

That's more than 160 laps in an Olympic pool!

One way that tigers *are* like house cats is that they both sleep a lot! Tigers sleep about 16–20 hours a day, mostly during the daytime. Why do tigers snooze so much? It's a super way to store up their energy. All that hunting, roaring, and swimming takes a lot of work!

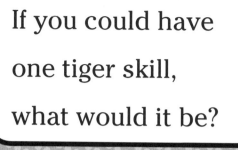

If you could have one tiger skill, what would it be?

Would you like to jump 30 feet . . . camouflage in the grass. . . or maybe sleep 20 hours a day?

Tigers are super in so many ways, but the coolest thing about them is . . . up to you!

Turn the page to learn about why tigers are disappearing, and how you can help!

Tigers are endangered (say: en-DAYNE-jurd). That means that they are in danger of becoming extinct (say: EX-tinkt) and disappearing forever. In fact, some tiger species have already gone extinct. Scientists think that the South China tiger no longer exists in the wild, although a few still live in zoos and protected nature reserves.

There are less than 4,000 tigers left in the wild. Why? People hunt and kill tigers, even though it is illegal. They also destroy the tigers' habitats by cutting down trees or by moving onto their land.

How can you help tigers?

People cut down trees from tiger habitats to make paper products. You can use less paper by using reusable shopping bags, lunch boxes, cups, and plates. If you must use paper, look for products made from recycled paper, which are made from paper that has already been used before. Your actions can help a super tiger!

GLOSSARY

cartilage: a soft material that human ears and noses, and shark skeletons, are made of

filter: to sort out

gills: organs that act as a fish's lungs and help it breathe underwater

lateral line: a system of organs that allows sharks to sense pressure and movement in the water

plankton: tiny plants and animals that float in lakes, rivers, and oceans

predator: an animal that hunts, kills, and eats other animals

prey: an animal hunted by a predator

reef: strips of coral, rock, or sand that are located in shallow water near coasts

scales: a bony material on the outside of shark and fish bodies

skeleton: a bony structure inside humans and other animals

snout: the part of an animal's face that includes its nose, mouth, and jaws

swell: to grow bigger

Note to readers: Some of these words may have more than one definition. The definitions above match how these words are used in this book.

Sharks can't smile, but can they live for hundreds of years?

How are sharks like human ears?

WOW!

By the time you get to the end of this book, you'll know the answers to these questions and more about what makes sharks super!

CHAPTER 1
SHARKS, SHARKS, EVERYWHERE!

There are more than 500 different kinds of sharks. They live in every ocean in the world and in some lakes and rivers.

Sharks are often named for what makes them special.

Young tiger sharks have stripes on their skin.

Saw sharks have snouts like saws.

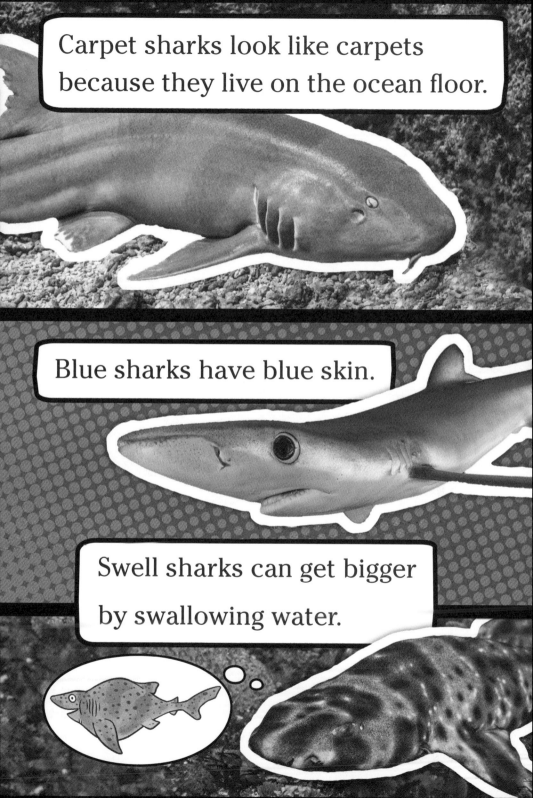

Carpet sharks look like carpets because they live on the ocean floor.

Blue sharks have blue skin.

Swell sharks can get bigger by swallowing water.

Sharks also come in all sizes.

American pocket sharks are shorter than a new pencil.

Whale sharks can be longer than a school bus!

American pocket shark: about 5 1/2 inches long

new number 2 pencil: 7 1/2 inches long

shortfin mako shark: up to nearly 13 feet long

megamouth shark: up to 17 feet long

great white shark: up to more than 20 feet long

school bus: up to 45 feet long

whale shark: up to 59 feet long

All sharks are predators (say: PRED-uh-turz). That means they hunt and eat other animals called prey (say: PRAY). Different sharks eat different prey. Some even eat other sharks!

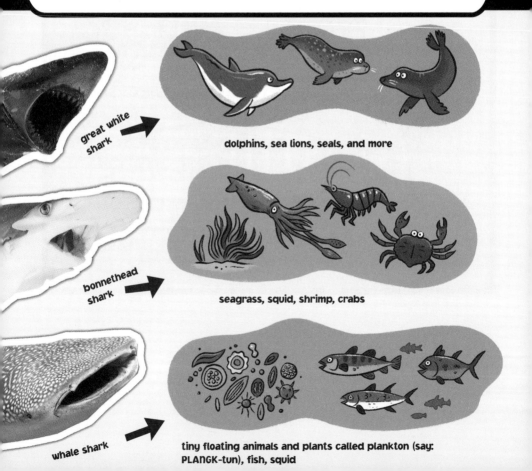

great white shark → dolphins, sea lions, seals, and more

bonnethead shark → seagrass, squid, shrimp, crabs

whale shark → tiny floating animals and plants called plankton (say: PLANGK-tun), fish, squid

Basking sharks swim with their mouths open to let in water. Then their body filters, or sorts out, the food in the water so they can eat it.

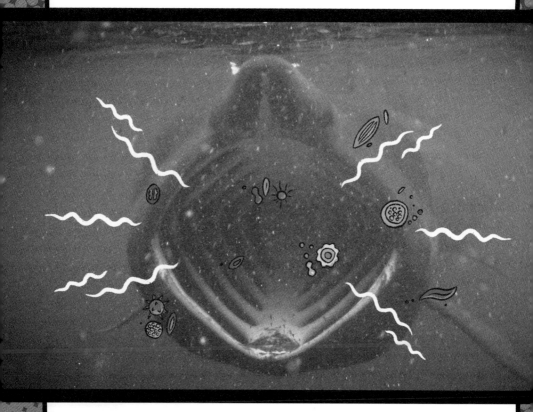

Whatever and however they eat, every shark loves a good meal!

Sharks have many powers that make them special.

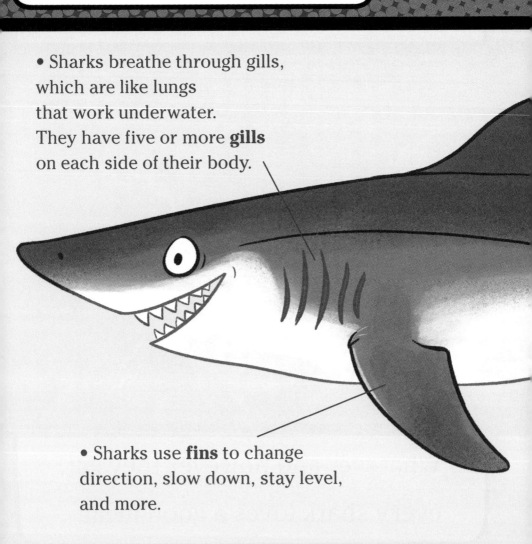

- Sharks breathe through gills, which are like lungs that work underwater. They have five or more **gills** on each side of their body.

- Sharks use **fins** to change direction, slow down, stay level, and more.

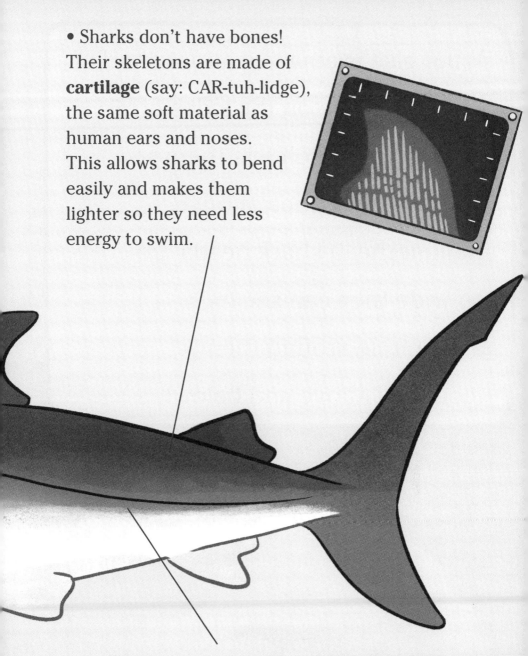

• Sharks don't have bones!
Their skeletons are made of
cartilage (say: CAR-tuh-lidge),
the same soft material as
human ears and noses.
This allows sharks to bend
easily and makes them
lighter so they need less
energy to swim.

• Sharks have a **lateral**
(say: LAT-ur-ull) **line**, a system
of organs in their body that senses
pressure and movement in water.

What else is amazing about sharks? Their eyes are on the sides of their head, which lets them see in many directions at once. Hammerhead shark heads are so wide they can see in a full circle around them, including above and below!

hammerhead shark

Many sharks protect their eyes with an extra clear eyelid. Great white sharks protect their eyes by rolling them back into their head!

That's not the only cool thing about shark eyes. They also seem to glow in the dark! A layer inside shines like a mirror when light hits it. This helps sharks see 10 or more times farther than humans can in low light.

Boo!

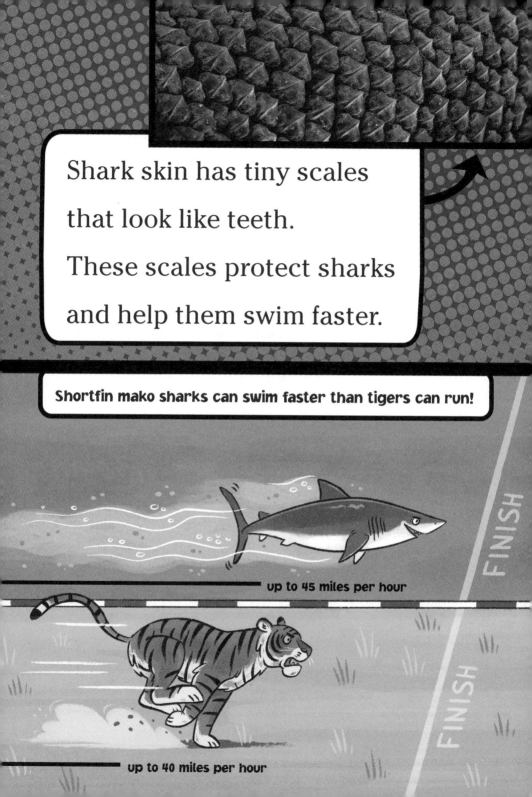

Shark skin has tiny scales that look like teeth. These scales protect sharks and help them swim faster.

Shortfin mako sharks can swim faster than tigers can run!

up to 45 miles per hour

FINISH

up to 40 miles per hour

FINISH

What beats swimming fast?

An amazing sense of smell!

Some sharks can smell one drop of blood in 10 billion drops of water. That's about as many drops needed to fill a swimming pool.

Leopard sharks know which direction a scent is coming from based on which nostril (say: NOSS-truhll) it reaches first.

Sharks also have a special sense that allows them to detect the heartbeats of nearby animals, even if the animals are hiding. How awesome is that?

SHARKS CAN'T SMILE . . . AND OTHER STRANGE FACTS

Sharks don't have the muscles needed to smile, but if they did, they would show off many rows of teeth.

Great white sharks can grow up to 20,000 teeth in their lifetime to replace any that they lose.

Shark teeth can be long, short, wide, thin, curved, or pointy, but they are not used for chewing.

Most sharks use teeth to bite . . .

and then they swallow food whole!

sand tiger shark

basking shark

Shark teeth have a coating that keeps them from getting cavities!

Speaking of teeth, sharks can open their mouths really wide because they can move both their upper and lower jaws, unlike humans.

They often take a sample bite of prey to make sure it is good to eat.

When a shark eats something by mistake that's not food, sometimes it has a gross way of spitting it out. The shark's stomach comes out of its body through its mouth and turns inside out!

What is stranger than that?

A shark that lives forever . . . almost!

Scientists believe Greenland sharks

can live for many hundreds of years.

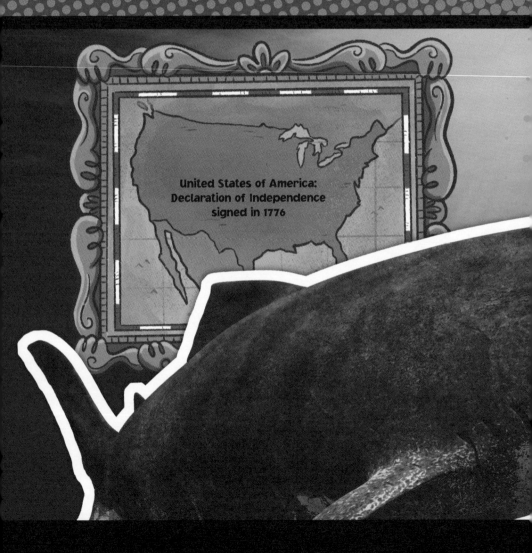

United States of America:
Declaration of Independence
signed in 1776

That means a Greenland shark that's alive today could have been born before the Declaration of Independence of the United States was signed on July 4, 1776!

oldest Greenland sharks: likely born long before 1776

Can you imagine living for hundreds of years and never sleeping? Well, most sharks don't sleep! They have to move forward to breathe, so they can slow down, but never completely fall asleep. Sharks also can't swim backward.

Epaulette (say: EH-puh-let) sharks have an amazing way of breathing if they get stuck on dry land or reefs.

They slow down their heart, lungs, and brain, and can live for an hour on one breath!
Then they use their fins like feet to walk back to the water!

If you could be like a shark,

would you want many rows of teeth

or to glow in the dark?

Would you want your bones to bend

like your ears do?

The coolest thing about sharks is . . .

up to you!

Turn the page to learn about why we
need to protect sharks!

PREDATORS NEED PROTECTION

Some people think sharks are not in danger of dying out because they are predators, but this is not true. Every year, humans kill up to 100 million sharks, often because of fishing. Sharks also get caught in fishing nets meant for other kinds of fish.

The world needs sharks to keep oceans healthy and balanced. Without sharks, their prey could take over and eat all the food in an area. Then, without any food, all the fish could die out. Without smaller fish to eat plants like algae (say: AL-jee), plants can grow so much that they block sunlight, putting animals that live in coral reefs in danger, and so on.

You can help sharks every day by using a reusable water bottle instead of plastic bottles that are only used once. A lot of plastic ends up in the ocean. It can hurt, or even kill animals if they eat or get tangled up in it. You can help by making sure to never leave trash on the beach. Keeping the ocean healthy starts with sharks . . . and you!

GLOSSARY

absorb: to take in or soak up

blubber: a special kind of fat that ocean mammals have underneath their skin that helps keep them warm

carnivores: animals that eat mostly meat instead of plants

marine animals: animals that need to live near the ocean to survive and that get most of their food from the ocean

predator: an animal that hunts, kills, and eats other animals

prey: an animal hunted by a predator

reflects: bounces off, such as light bouncing off a mirror

sleuth: a group of bears

Note to readers: Some of these words may have more than one definition. The definitions above match how these words are used in this book.

Polar bears are super!
How do their paws help them
swim fast and walk on ice?
Why do they roll in snow
or touch noses?

Why does their fur look white, and what color is it really? By the time you get to the end of this book, you'll know all about what makes polar bears amazing!

My fur sure looks *white* to me!

CHAPTER 1
MARINE BEARS

Polar bears are marine

(say: muh-REEN) animals,

which means they need to live near

the ocean to survive in the wild.

They are the only
marine bears.

Polar bears live in the Arctic, the area around the Earth's North Pole. The water is so cold there that a lot of the surface, or top, is frozen. Ice is no problem for polar bears, though!

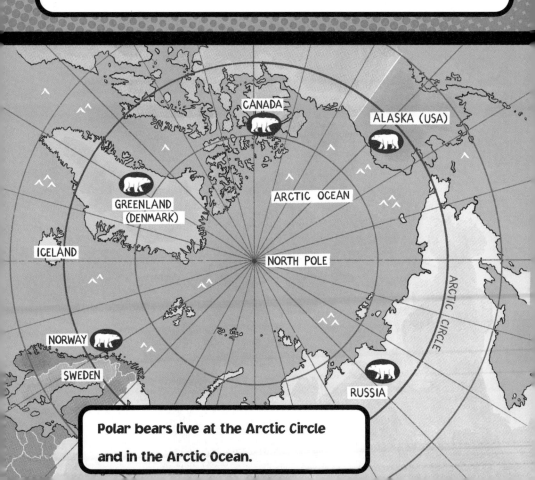

Polar bears live at the Arctic Circle and in the Arctic Ocean.

Polar bears are predators
(say: PRED-uh-ters), which means
they hunt and eat other animals.
The animals that predators eat are
called prey (say: PRAY).
Polar bears mostly eat seals.
Seals have a lot of blubber.

Polar Bear

Ringed Seal

Fish

Arctic Shrimp

Algae

Blubber is a special kind of fat that helps marine animals store energy, stay warm, and float more easily! If a polar bear can't find seals to eat, it will eat reindeer, rodents, seaweed, and just about anything else! Polar bears can survive without food for up to 240 days.

Sometimes, if a polar bear is hungry, it will ask another polar bear to share its meal. It asks by touching noses with the other polar bear!

Polar bears also touch noses to greet each other. While they spend a lot of time alone, when polar bears are in a group, they are called a sleuth (say: SLOOTH) of polar bears!

Can I have some?

Sure! My seal is your seal!

Polar bears are the largest carnivores (say: KAR-nuh-vores), or animals that eat meat, that live on land.

And they call YOU the KING of the beasts?

SUPER!

POLAR BEARS

Nearly nine feet long and up to **1,600** pounds

LIONS

Nearly nine feet long and up to **500** pounds

Even so, when they are born, polar bear cubs are very small at around 12 inches long. That is as long as a ruler, or an adult guinea pig!

Before cubs are born, their mother makes a snow den by digging a cave in the snow. Mothers usually give birth in the snow den, and often have twins!

Newborn cubs cannot see or hear. They stay in the warm den with their mother until they're about 4 months old.

CHAPTER 2

WARM AND FAST BEARS!

In the winter, the temperature in the Arctic is often way below freezing. Luckily, polar bears have about 4 inches of blubber under their skin that helps them stay warm. Sometimes they have to dive into icy water to cool off!

The blubber keeps the bears from losing heat from their bodies. So little heat escapes that if you used a special video camera that "sees" only heat, polar bears would be almost invisible!

Polar bears have other cool abilities. Their huge paws help them walk on top of thin ice and deep snow.

Like snowshoes that humans wear, the big paws spread out the bear's weight and put less pressure on the snow or ice below.

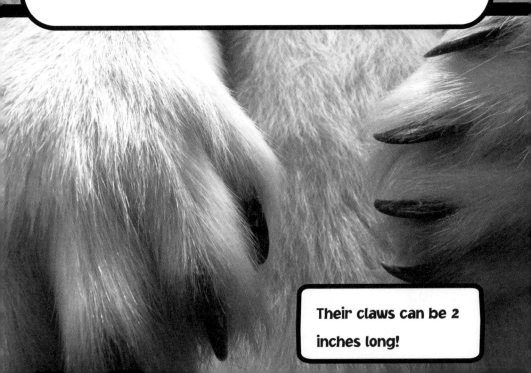

Their claws can be 2 inches long!

The bottoms of their paws have another amazing feature. They have small, soft bumps that grip the ice.

What is pizza?

A polar bear's paw is about 12 inches in diameter—about the same size as a medium pizza.

Another fun fact about feet?
Polar bear paws have glands that
leave behind a scent that helps
polar bears find one another.
This is possible because polar bears
have an excellent sense of smell.
On land, they can smell a seal
from 20 miles away.

They can also smell a seal in the water, even when the seal is swimming under more than 3 feet of ice and snow.

That's not all! Polar bears can swim at speeds of about 6 miles per hour. That's the same speed as Olympic swimming champion Michael Phelps! Polar bears have webbing between their toes, so their feet act like flippers to make them swim faster!

Their back legs help them change direction when they swim, similar to the rudder on a ship.

Polar bears can also run at speeds of up to 25 miles per hour on land. Most of the time, though, polar bears sit still at seal breathing holes, waiting for seals to appear.

Their nostrils close up underwater.

They have webbed feet.

In addition to blubber, thick fur helps polar bears stay warm.

Clean fur does the best job of keeping out the cold.

How does a polar bear keep its fur clean?

By rolling in snow!

It's like taking a snow bath!

A polar bear's top layer of fur is hollow, which means each hair has an open space in the middle of it. The hollow space inside the fur traps body heat and helps keep the polar bear warm!

My fur is **Clear**?

Polar bear fur looks white, which makes them blend in with white snow when they hunt. If you looked under a microscope, you would see that up close their fur is clear, with no color at all. Objects look the color they do because of how light reflects, or bounces, off the object.

A rainbow contains all of the visible colors.

Sunlight looks white. When sunlight hits polar bear fur, the white light bounces around the hollow space inside each hair and then bounces back out again. The white light makes clear polar bear fur look white too.

Underneath the fur, polar bear skin is black. Something looks black when all the colors of sunlight are absorbed and none are reflected. This helps black objects absorb more heat from sunlight too. The color of polar bear skin makes it easier for the bears to stay warm.

If you could be like a polar bear, would you like to stay so warm that you wouldn't ever need a jacket?

Would you want to have feet that work like snowshoes and flippers?

Polar bears are really neat, but what do you think is the most interesting thing about them? The choice is yours!

Turn the page to learn about how protecting the planet can help polar bears, too!

SAVE POLAR BEARS, SAVE THE WORLD

Unfortunately, the number of polar bears in the world is dropping, in part because Earth's climate is getting hotter. Climate is the average measurement of temperature, wind, rain, and snow in a place over time. The climate where polar bears live is getting warmer more quickly than at any other time in history. This is causing sea ice to melt.

Scientists believe that climate change is happening because of human activities, like burning fuel and cutting down trees, which increase the amount of carbon dioxide in Earth's atmosphere. Carbon dioxide traps heat and causes high temperatures.

You can help slow down climate change every day by saving energy. Turn off the lights when you leave a room, and ask your family to try walking instead of taking the car when you're not going very far. Plant a tree, if you can. By being thoughtful today, you can make the world a better place for polar bears—and humans!

GLOSSARY

cold-blooded: having a body temperature that matches the temperature of its surroundings

constrictor: a snake that coils around its prey and squeezes it to death

habitat: a place where an animal lives in nature

ligament: a tough band of tissue that connects one bone to another

predator: an animal that hunts, kills, and eats other animals

prey: an animal hunted by a predator for food

reptile: a cold-blooded animal whose body is usually covered in scales or bony plates

shed: to grow out of and lose, such as an outgrown skin

species: a specific kind of animal or plant

venom: a type of poison that one animal injects into another animal

Note to readers: Some of these words may have more than one definition. The definitions above match how these words are used in this book.

Did you know that some snakes climb trees and that others swim, or glide through the air?

Did you know that snakes hear with their jawbones and smell with their tongues?

By the time you finish this book, you'll know all about what makes snakes so sssssuper!

CHAPTER 1

SO MANY SNAKES!

There are more than 3,000 species (say: SPEE-shees), or kinds, of snakes.

The red diamond rattlesnake lives in the Southern California mountains and deserts, and on some islands.

NORTH AMERICA

SOUTH AMERICA

The yellow-bellied sea snake swims in the open ocean.

They live in most types of habitats (say: HAB-eh-TATS), from warm, tropical places to deserts—and oceans.

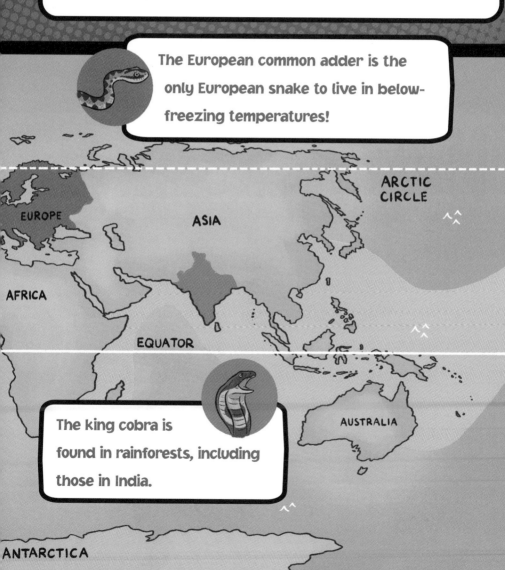

The European common adder is the only European snake to live in below-freezing temperatures!

ARCTIC CIRCLE

EUROPE

ASIA

AFRICA

EQUATOR

The king cobra is found in rainforests, including those in India.

AUSTRALIA

ANTARCTICA

Snakes come in all different sizes, colors, and patterns too. They are commonly divided into two categories: ones with venom and ones without.

Nonvenomous Snakes

(say: non-VEN-um-us)

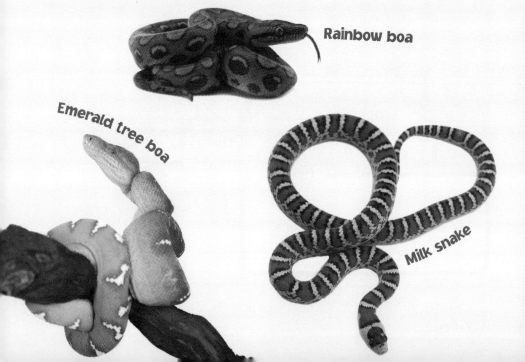

Rainbow boa

Emerald tree boa

Milk snake

Venom (say: VEN-um) is a poison that one animal injects into another animal.

Venomous Snakes

Copperhead

King cobra

Inland taipan

The coral snake has bright colors to warn other animals to steer clear!

A venomous snake bites its prey (say: PRAY) and, through its fangs, injects the prey with venom. The venom stuns or kills the prey.

All snakes are reptiles (say: REP-tyles). They have scaly skin and are cold-blooded animals that lie in the sun to get warm, and go into the shade or the water to keep cool.

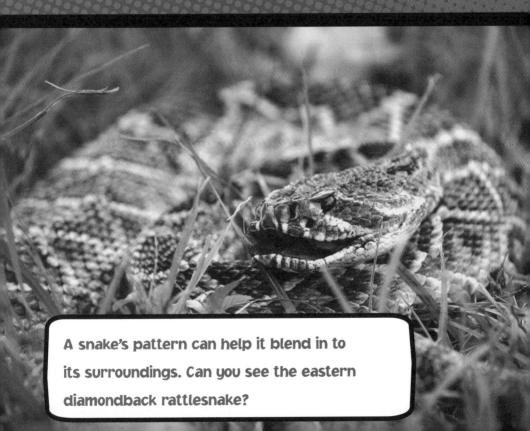

A snake's pattern can help it blend in to its surroundings. Can you see the eastern diamondback rattlesnake?

CHAPTER 2

HISS AND TELL

A snake keeps growing for its entire life. But its skin doesn't!

Right before it sheds its skin, a snake's eyes turn milky blue!

So a snake sheds or loses its skin several times a year.

A snake slithers out of its old skin headfirst.

Ahh! Much better!

A snake rubs against something to help shed its old skin.

Snakes range in size from 4 inches to over 20 feet! A reticulated (say: rah-TIC-you-LAY-ted) python can be up to 32 feet long—over 90 times longer than the Barbados (say: bar-BAY-dose) threadsnake!

Heavyweight champion! An anaconda

(say: AN-a-con-da) can weigh up to 550 pounds!

Flick! A snake moves its tongue through the air. The tongue picks up tiny amounts of odors from the snake's surroundings and carries them to the roof of the snake's mouth. And that's how a snake smells things!

A snake manages to hear through the bones in its lower jaw. The bones pick up vibrations of moving things and send messages about them to the snake's brain.

Those are some good vibrations!

Snakes have no external ears!

All snakes are predators
(say: PRED-uh-ters) that hunt
and eat prey.
Some snakes grab prey with their
teeth and swallow the prey alive.

The king cobra eats small animals
but has enough venom to kill an
elephant!

Other snakes are constrictors (say: cun-STRICT-ers). A constrictor grabs prey and wraps its body around the animal. The constrictor restricts their prey's blood flow until it dies, and then eats it.

Boas and other constrictors squeeze their prey to death, but no bones get broken!

All snakes' teeth face inward and keep prey from being able to escape.

All snakes swallow their prey whole. And thanks to ligaments (say: LIG-uh-mints)—which are tough bands of tissue—in the jaw that *s-t-r-e-t-c-h*, a snake can swallow prey 3 times larger than its head!

The bigger the snake, the bigger the meal it can swallow. A python regularly eats about one quarter of its body weight at once, but sometimes swallows things larger than itself!

Want to eat as much as a python? You'll have to chow down on **240** quarter-pound cheeseburgers!

CHAPTER 3

THAT'S REALLY MOVING!

The black mamba has been clocked speeding along at 12 1/2 miles per hour. That may not seem terribly fast, but it's pretty impressive for a creature slithering on its belly!

Human: up to 27.8 miles per hour

0 mph · 5 mph · 10 mph · mph · 25 mph · 30 r

Black mamba: up to 12.5 miles per hour

Blink and you've missed it. What? In the amount of time it takes a person to blink once, a western diamondback rattlesnake can strike at prey 4 times!

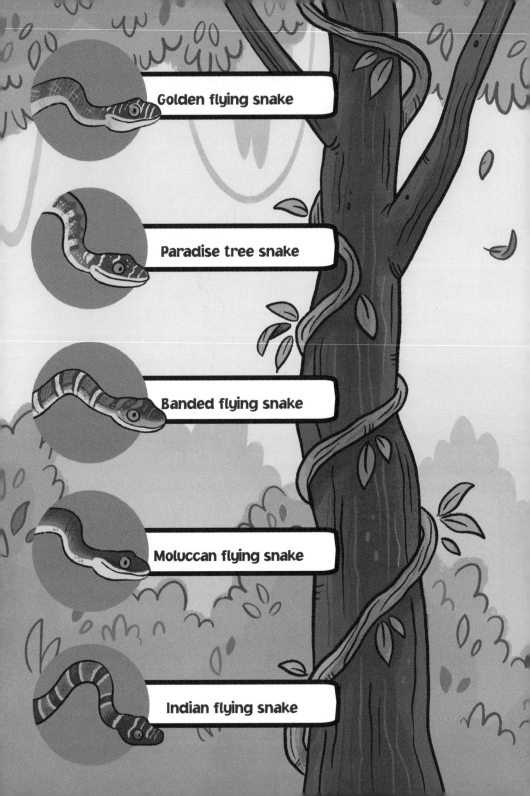

Golden flying snake

Paradise tree snake

Banded flying snake

Moluccan flying snake

Indian flying snake

Some snakes live mostly in trees, and when they need to move, they just glide through the air!

To glide through the air, a snake flattens its ribs into a C shape and then moves its body in S-shaped waves.

Other snakes live in the sea, where their oar-like tails help them swim!

A sea snake dives to the seafloor to find food.

Say what? Some scientists believe that snakes have friends!
Studies of eastern garter snakes show that they look for other snakes to hang out with—and are picky about it!

If you could be a snake, would you like to move on land, through the air, or in water?

Would you like to smell things with your tongue and hear things with your jaw?

There are so many awesome things about snakes! What is your favorite thing that a snake can do?

Turn the page to learn some more very surprising facts about snakes!

There are about 600 species of venomous snakes in the world, of which about 200 can kill or seriously hurt humans. But scientists also know that snake venom can be made into medicines that can save or help human lives! Since 1981, venom from the Brazilian pit viper has been used in a blood pressure medicine that is commonly prescribed worldwide. Two medicines based on snake venom that help treat heart conditions were approved in the late 1990s. And now scientists are studying how snake venom may be used in even more medicines. One team is working with king cobra venom to see how it might be developed into an effective painkiller. More than 100 other snake venoms, including that of the Iranian spider-tailed viper, are also being studied to see how they might help stop dangerous blood clots. Snakes are not just super—some can be *super*heroes!

GLOSSARY

apex predator: an animal that is not eaten or hunted by other animals in the wild

brackish water: water that is saltier than fresh water but not as salty as salt water

caiman: a crocodilian that is very closely related to alligators

cold-blooded: having a body temperature that matches the temperature of its surroundings

crocodilians: a group of animal species including crocodiles, alligators, caimans, and gharials; all crocodilians have powerful bites, many teeth, short legs, webbed back feet, long tails, and thick bony-plated skin

endangered: at risk of disappearing forever

gharial: a crocodilian with a long, thin snout

keystone species: an animal or plant that helps other animals and plants survive in the same area

prey: an animal hunted by a predator

reptile: a cold-blooded animal whose body is usually covered in scales or bony plates

wetland: a place where the ground is soft, wet, and often flooded; swamps and marshes are different kinds of wetlands

Note to readers: Some of these words may have more than one definition. The definitions above match how these words are used in this book.

Did you know that alligators and crocodiles have some of the strongest bites in the world? They might have an impressive bite, but they actually can't chew!

By the time you finish this book, you'll know a lot of amazing facts about alligators and crocodiles!

SNAP!

CHAPTER 1

IS IT AN ALLIGATOR OR A CROCODILE?

Both alligators and crocodiles

are crocodilians

(say: krah-kuh-DIH-lee-uhns).

alligators

caimans

(say: KAY-muhns) are

crocodilians that are very

similar to alligators.

Crocodilians are a group of animals with long tails, short legs, webbed back feet, many pointed teeth, and thick bony-plated skin.

crocodilians

gharials
(say: GAIR-ee-uhls) have long, thin snouts.

crocodiles

How can you tell an alligator from a crocodile?

One way is to look at the snout!

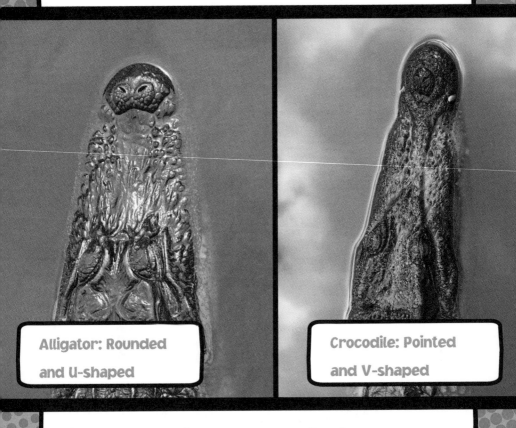

Alligator: Rounded and U-shaped

Crocodile: Pointed and V-shaped

Alligators have rounded snouts and crocodiles have pointed snouts.

If you see only

the animal's top teeth

when the mouth is closed,

the animal is an alligator.

If you see top and bottom teeth

when the mouth is closed,

it's a crocodile.

Alligators live in wetlands with soft and wet ground, near freshwater lakes and rivers.

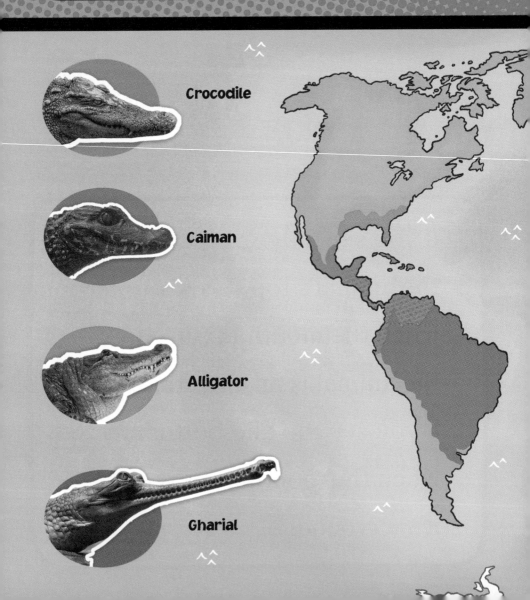

Crocodile

Caiman

Alligator

Gharial

Most crocodiles live in salt water or brackish (say: BRAK-ish) water, which is saltier than fresh water but not as salty as salt water.

South Florida is the only place in the wild where alligators and crocodiles both live.

Most crocodiles are also larger than alligators.

Cuvier's dwarf caiman: about 5 feet

American alligator: about 11 feet

four standard shopping carts: about 12 feet

American crocodile: about 15 feet

saltwater crocodile: up to 23 feet

One thing that crocodiles and alligators do have in common is that they can climb trees! Scientists think they climb to warm up their bodies and to check out their surroundings. Now you can be an expert at spotting alligators and crocodiles!

CHAPTER 2

IN AND OUT OF THE WATER

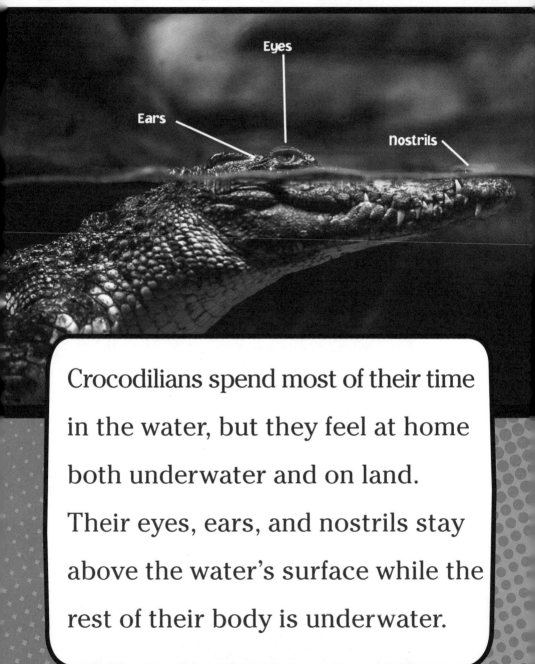

Eyes

Ears

Nostrils

Crocodilians spend most of their time in the water, but they feel at home both underwater and on land. Their eyes, ears, and nostrils stay above the water's surface while the rest of their body is underwater.

When it's time to dive, crocodilians have things covered . . . literally!

Crocodilians can stay underwater for 2 hours!

Ears and nostrils close tight to keep water from entering.

Special eyelids protect their eyes so that they can see underwater.

A special flap at the back of the throat keeps water out.

When a crocodilian crawls onto land, its webbed feet help it move through muddy, shallow water. Then it lies in the sun to warm up.

Crocodilians are cold-blooded reptiles. This means their body temperatures match the temperature outside.

If they get hot, crocodilians open their mouths to cool off. Reptiles can't sweat!

Female crocodilians go on land to lay eggs. They may lay as many as 90 eggs at once!

The temperature of the nest decides if the babies are female or male.

91.4 degrees Fahrenheit and above: Most American alligator babies are male.

°F

86 degrees Fahrenheit and below: Most American alligator babies are female.

Once the babies hatch, the mother gently scoops up to 15 newborns at a time into her mouth and carries them to the water.

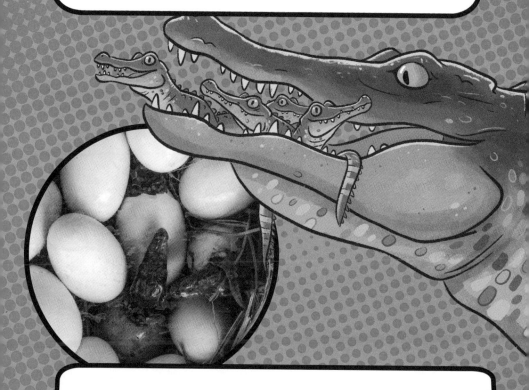

The babies will grow up both in water and on land.

CHAPTER 3
FEARSOME PREDATORS

Crocodilians can slam their jaws shut 6 times faster than you can blink. Their bite forces are some of the strongest in the world.

Some Bite Strengths to Chew On...

HUMAN
ABOUT 160 PSI
(POUNDS PER SQUARE INCH)

LION
ABOUT 1,000 PSI

However, crocodilians can't chew! They don't have the muscles to move their jaws like that.

Pounds per square inch (psi) is a unit used to measure the amount of pressure placed on something.

SALTWATER CROCODILE ABOUT 3,700 PSI

If crocodilians can't chew,
how do they eat?
They swallow small animals whole
and use their sharp teeth
to break apart larger ones.

They also swallow stones, which stay in their stomachs and help grind up food.

Crocodilians digest their food slowly. Some can go without eating for a year!

Crocodilians are fierce animals that hunt and eat other animals called prey (say: PRAY).
They eat all kinds of prey, including fish, frogs, birds, deer, and even other crocodilians!

Some crocodilians are
apex predators
(say: AY-pecks PRED-uh-turs).
This means that
they aren't hunted or eaten
by other animals in the wild.

While American alligators are hungry predators, they also help other animals. They dig big holes in the ground to create small ponds. When the dry season comes, the alligator holes are rare sources of water until the wet season starts again.

Other animals use the holes for water too. The alligator eats some of these animals, but most are able to stay alive. Because other animals depend on the American alligator to survive, it is called a keystone species (say: KEE-stoen SPEE-sheez).

If you could be like a crocodilian, what would you want to do?

Would you want to grow a long tail, stay underwater for 2 hours, or quickly snap your jaws shut?

Whatever you decide,
one thing is for certain:
alligators and crocodiles
are amazing!

Turn the page to learn about protecting alligators

SAVE ALLIGATORS AND CROCODILES, SAVE THE WORLD

Many crocodilians are endangered, which means they are at risk of disappearing forever. This is because people hunt them for food and for their skin. People are also destroying and moving into the areas where crocodilians live.

In the 1960s, the American alligator population was quickly disappearing. The American government passed laws that made it illegal to hunt alligators. They also protected alligator land and started a breeding program. Thanks to these efforts, the American alligator is no longer endangered. This success story provides hope for other endangered crocodilians.

How can you help alligators and crocodiles?

Tell your family and friends not to buy clothes and other items made from animal skin. If you live near a wetland, you can volunteer to help clean up garbage that can hurt the animals living there. Your actions can help a super crocodilian!